COLETTE BARON-REID

ORACLE *of the* 7
ENERGIES
Journal

HAY HOUSE, INC.
Carlsbad, California • New York City
London • Sydney • New Delhi

THIS JOURNAL BELONGS TO:

_____

Published in the United States by: Hay House, Inc.: www.hayhouse .com® • **Published in Australia by:** Hay House Australia Pty. Ltd.: www.hayhouse.com.au • **Published in the United Kingdom by:** Hay House UK, Ltd.: www.hayhouse.co.uk • **Published in India by:** Hay House Publishers India: www.hayhouse.co.in

Original artwork: Jena DellaGrottaglia • *Art direction & design:* Brooke Vreeland • *Concept:* Colette Baron-Reid and ElizaBeth Fincannon Wilson • Special thanks to Michele Rosario for your wonderful contribution and support.

ISBN: 978-1-4019-6291-3

10 9 8 7 6 5 4 3 2 1
1st edition, October 2020

Printed in the United States of America

CONTENTS

WELCOME

The concept of the seven energies can be said
to apply to the totality of your life's story—the way
you think, how you make your choices, and what you
encounter within yourself—and the conditions
of your world as you journey forward.

WORKING WITH THE

ORACLE *of the* 7 ENERGIES

Journal

Welcome to your *Oracle of the 7 Energies Journal*! This unique journal was created as a companion to the *Oracle of the 7 Energies* deck to give you a space to reflect on the oracle cards you pull, inspire you to explore the themes of each energy center and how they relate to your life, and give you a safe place to activate your creativity as you dive deeper into the essence of each of these energies.

There's no right or wrong way to use this journal. You can use it as a diary to explore your thoughts and feelings or as a place to record and reflect on your oracle card readings, write gratitude notes, or doodle and create on the blank pages. The possibilities are endless!

If you do find yourself needing a little guidance for how to fill your journal, I've included affirmations, writing prompts, and creative exploration exercises for each of the energies. Use any of these as a starting point for journaling or drawing.

Each energy includes a description of its key concepts as well as its corresponding element, color, and musical note. I hope that this inspires you to play with the concept of the seven energies as you go along. Allow your creativity to guide you as to what you'd like to do. You might want to create art or wear a particular energy's color, or use a tuning fork or musical instrument to play the note. To learn more about each element and your relationship to its theme, you can divide the cards in your *Oracle of the 7 Energies* deck by the separate elements and do a reading with only the cards of your chosen element.

Additionally, in the back of the journal, you will find ideas for one-, two-, and three-card oracle card spreads, as well as an exclusive series of guided meditations for each of the seven energies.

I really loved creating this journal for you, and I hope it serves you well. If you'd like to share how you've used the journal or the art you've created on your blank pages, I'd love for you to send me pictures and messages. You can e-mail me at journal@colettebaronreid.com or share photos on social media with the hashtag #7EnergiesJournal.

With bushels of blessings and magical wishes,

- Colette

ENERGY 1

Key concepts: money, family, inherited traits, survival,
primitive instincts, security, stability,
and the material world

Element: Earth | Rainbow Color: Red | Musical Note: C

ENERGY 1 - AFFIRMATIONS

I quiet my thoughts and imagine anchoring my energy to the sacred quality of being part of this living earth.

Growth never follows a straight line; I will manifest what I need when I need it.

It's time to put myself first. Then everything will fall beautifully into place.

I ask for courage to take a leap into the unknown, and I know that all will be well.

Real transformation can happen once I surrender to the idea that things are exactly as they are meant to be.

I'm invited to surrender to an important truth: there is always enough for me.

Life loves me.

My life is brimming with unique potential—I focus on that!

Today, I choose love over fear. I'll be amazed when I do.

When I release my attachment to getting what I want, I'll be surprised by how much energy I have for more important things.

ENERGY 1 - WRITING PROMPTS

What makes you feel most grounded and rooted in the physical world? What makes you feel disconnected? Why?

What will it take for you to feel safe and secure? Is it money? Love? Something else?

How can you better take in the beauty of your life in the present moment?

What are you grateful for? Why?

How do you love the part of you that's afraid? How can you show more compassion?

Visualize your most grateful self. Imagine the way you walk, speak, and treat others. See in your mind what you look like with full confidence. How does this differ from who you are now?

Write down your fears—small ones, big ones. How do you think these fears affect who you are in the present moment?

How do you practice extreme self-care?

ENERGY 1 – CREATIVE EXPLORATION

Use a blank page in this journal to draw whatever you want. Draw what makes you feel good, and what feels right. Can you accept what you have drawn, or do you criticize it?

Create an altar or nature table for natural objects. If you've got a collection of beautiful objects from nature—stones, flowers, seashells, etc.—add them to this little designated area so that you are reminded every day to connect with the elements.

Go out in nature and plant your bare feet into the grass, the sand, the dirt, etc. Feel your feet connecting with the vibration of Earth's energy.

To connect to the grounded energy of Earth, hold a natural object in your hands such as a stone, a branch, a flower, or a pinecone. Allow yourself to tune in to this object and really connect with its energy.

Spend some time in a natural area or walking around your neighborhood cleaning up trash to show love and respect to Mother Earth!

You know the saying "dance like nobody's watching"? That's exactly what you're going to do! Put on your favorite high-energy, feel-good song and turn it up! Let your body move naturally to the rhythm of the music. Don't think about the movements you're making; just close your eyes and move. If you're able to, stomp your feet emphatically into the ground! Repeat this exercise any time you feel a need to reconnect with your body and ground yourself.

ENERGY 2

Key concepts: connection, sexuality,
intimacy, birthing, desire, pleasure,
feelings, and fluidity

Element: Water | Rainbow Color: Orange | Musical Note: D

ENERGY 2 - AFFIRMATIONS

Intimate relationships hold up a mirror of truth to me and reveal more treasures than I might ever expect.

I lower my shields and allow myself to step into a dance of intimacy.

I am a note in a harmony that neither overpowers nor is overpowered by any other.

I trust my instincts and take care of myself.

I am firm yet kind.

Pleasure is part of life; I let myself surrender to it today.

Now is the time for rigorous honesty as I take a self-inventory with a neutral state of mind.

Everything is intrinsically connected.

My empathy is beautiful and important.

I will discover more about who I am as I discover more about another.

ENERGY 2 - WRITING PROMPTS

What masks do you wear to protect yourself from building true intimacy with the rest of the world? What aspects of your true self are you afraid to allow to be seen? Why?

One of the most important partnerships you'll ever have is the partnership with your Higher Self—the aspect of you that is always in communion with the Spirit World and intuiting helpful guidance for your human experience. What guidance are you already receiving from your Higher Self every day? Do you heed this guidance or ignore it? Why?

Are you carrying any guilt around for anything you've previously experienced? What do you need in order to release this burden and no longer carry it with you?

How do you like to experience pleasure? What do you need to do to bring more pleasure into your life?

How do you honor the commitments you make to yourself? What does that look like? How do you experience it?

If your life were a tree, what fruit would it bear? Truly delve into this question! What are the fruits of your collective mental, spiritual, emotional, and physical labors? Are you happy with what is being brought forth from your unseen world into the material plane?

ENERGY 2 - CREATIVE EXPLORATION

Flip to one of the unlined pages in this journal or grab some paper; pick up some watercolors, crayons, or markers; and create a picture inspired by water. Let go of perfectionism! This process of creating is just for you to cultivate a connection to water.

Next time you have a meal, totally drop into the experience of eating it for at least a minute. Really be there with your meal and tune in to it. What do you hear as you eat? What do you smell and taste? What do you see? What does the texture of the food feel like as you chew? This is a simple way to pull your awareness into your physical body and connect with the pleasurable sensations of enjoying a meal.

Next time you are in the shower, close your eyes and imagine that the water is made of beautiful, golden light. As it pours down onto you and cleanses your physical body, also visualize how it washes away any dark spots in your auric field—the energy surrounding your physical body—and replaces any dark spots with the light of the perfect vibration and frequency for your health and well-being. All exhausted energy pours down into the drain and back into Earth, where it will be transformed and reused. Don't worry if you struggle with visualizing the whole process. Just intend that the shower be healing and trust that Source and your Higher Self will support and facilitate the process.

What better way to promote flexibility and the watery, "go with the flow" mindset than stretching your physical body or practicing a gentle yoga flow? Even if you can only dedicate 5 to 10 minutes out of your day, this will make a difference. Find what feels good for you and go with the flow!

ENERGY 3

Key concepts: personal power, will, assertiveness, action, vitality, movement, individuation, and extreme states—joy, anger, transformation

Element: Fire | Rainbow Color: Yellow | Musical Note: E

ENERGY 3 - AFFIRMATIONS

I am a mighty co-creator.

Now is the time for me to lead from my personal power.

I am the ruler of my mind.

It is important now to keep my focus on what is right and good for me as well as others.

I hold my head high and know my worth.

I am open and clear about my motives and desires, and I set my intention.

Once I recognize what story I'm telling others about how to treat me, I can tell a different one.

I let curiosity be the focus now.

All will be better than well.

I have everything I need to tell a new tale and weave more blessings in the world as my unique contribution.

ENERGY 3 - WRITING PROMPTS

Imagine that you have two Sovereigns that live inside you: One is the Illuminated Queen/King and holds all your most light-filled, acceptable, and beautiful qualities. The other is your Shadow Queen/King and has all the qualities that are deemed difficult or hard for you or society to accept. Much of our personal power is often hidden in these shadow qualities, and in order to use them constructively, we must identify and own them. Write a love letter to your shadow self, acknowledging and listing your "darker" qualities and reminding this self that you love them anyway.

In what ways do you allow creative self-expression in your life? In what ways do you block it?

Are there any stories in your life that you're tired of telling yourself and others? (Ex: *I'm not good enough because . . . , I can't do this because . . . , I always . . . , I never . . .*) What stories would you rather tell instead?

What are you most afraid of? How does that affect your life choices?

Consider a time in your life where you feel you gave your personal power away. Now rewrite that story, and instead, include details of how you handled it with assertiveness and demanded that your boundaries would be upheld.

Do you feel ashamed about anything in your life or past? If so, how is that affecting your life now? In what ways do you shame others?

ENERGY 3 - CREATIVE EXPLORATION

Flip to a blank page or grab some paper and some crayons, paint, charcoal, or whatever your favorite medium is and create a piece of art inspired by fire. The act of creating is fiery in itself as you ignite your creativity and vision. Let go of perfectionism! It doesn't have to be fine art! This process of creating is just for you to cultivate a connection to fire.

Find a cozy, sunny spot in your house or outside and just spend a few minutes with your eyes closed, soaking in the nourishment and magic of the sunshine. Send gratitude for the warmth and revitalization.

Sit with the element of fire—whether it's a bonfire in your backyard, beach, or campground; a candle in your house; a cozy flame in your fireplace; or even just a picture or image of fire—and allow yourself to just drop in with and connect with fire. What feelings come up? What messages do you hear?

Is there anything you wish to release and let go of? A grudge, a fixation with an experience, expectations, worries, doubts, fears? Write whatever you wish to let go of down on a piece of paper. When you're finished, set the intention of releasing and transmuting these things and no longer carrying them with you on your journey. In a safe place (such as a fireplace) burn this paper. Watch as the flames transform and transmute the paper that carries the energy of that which you choose to release. Let it go and thank this blessed element for its power of transformation.

ENERGY 4

Key concepts: compassion, love, community, forgiveness,
unconditional acceptance, inner peace,
and wholeness

Element: Love | Rainbow Color: Green | Musical Note: F

ENERGY 4 - AFFIRMATIONS

I release myself from the burdens of perfectionism.

Love is the strength I need today.

The only way forward is to move through it.

I look for ways I can help myself and others.

Compassion is an emotion of tenderness and sensitivity.

When I accept myself, I can bring more loving energy to others.

Now is the time for radical forgiveness.

I surrender to the magic I share.

It's time to do my part to sing in harmony with others.

I am being invited now to explore love in all its beauty.

ENERGY 4 - WRITING PROMPTS

Talk about your relationship with forgiveness. Does it come easily for you? Do you struggle with truly letting go and forgiving yourself or others? Why?

What does *Love* mean to you? When you tell someone that you love them, what are you truly trying to express to them?

Reflect on a time where you felt your heart was "broken" by an experience. Have you been able to move through it and find a blessing within it yet? If not, what keeps you stuck in the heartbreak?

Write a "love letter" to your inner child, telling this child (yourself) everything you needed to hear when you were little. Know that healing transcends time and space. Sending love to yourself as a child is a powerful way to heal old wounds and rewrite your inner stories.

Where in your life can you be kinder or gentler? In what ways do you already practice kindness and compassion? What holds you back from being vulnerable?

In what ways are you being called to serve the Collective from your heart with your own unique talents?

ENERGY 4 – CREATIVE EXPLORATION

Flip to a blank page in this journal or grab a piece of paper and something to draw with. Reflect on the key concepts of Energy 4 and what words come to mind for you. Use the words to create a word cloud in the shape of a flower, a heart, or other shapes that inspire you. It doesn't have to be perfect! Your word art is just for you, so have fun with your creation.

Flowers, especially roses, are a simple yet powerful symbol of love. When you need a simple way to open your heart, spend time working with flowers. Take a walk and notice the blooms, buy yourself a bouquet and make a pretty arrangement for your home, spend time gazing at or meditating with a flower, or find any way that feels natural for you to connect with the essence of flowers.

Close your eyes and take a few breaths. Drop into your body; in your heart space, take inventory of what the energy looks and feels like. Does it feel open, vibrant, and energized? Does it feel muddy, stagnant, or closed? Begin to envision a glowing ball of vibrant green light in your heart space. Focus on allowing this ball of green light to expand bigger and brighter until it encircles your entire body and nourishes all of your cells. When you feel like you've been energized enough, bring your awareness back into your body and into the room.

Our deepest and most heart-hardening wounds often stem from childhood experiences. Take some time to work with and engage your inner child; find an inner child meditation, play something you loved as a child, write affirmations you needed to hear as a child, or simply look in the mirror and say "I love you" to your inner child.

ENERGY 5

Key concepts: communication, creativity,
listening, being heard, writing, ideas,
sharing, and vibration

Element: Sound | Rainbow Color: Blue | Musical Note: G

ENERGY 5 - AFFIRMATIONS

When my genius awakens, I realize I do not have to do everything myself.

Deep listening is the way in which I immerse myself in the truth of the world.

I now commit to partnering with my genius.

It is my duty to share my gifts.

I take center stage, and I am noticed.

I have come so far.

Everything is perfect as it is.

Opportunities arise from the subtle cues I tune in to when I'm listening.

I hear and refuse the voices in my head that say *I can't*, *I'm unworthy*, or *I'm not good enough*.

The world is constantly speaking to me and offering clues about what is really going on beneath the surface of things.

ENERGY 5 - WRITING PROMPTS

What are some personal truths that you need to express right now?

What are some sources of media or information that you use in your daily life that are truly nourishing to your psyche and spirit? What are some sources that you use or visit daily that cause fear, anxiety, or any amount of discomfort in your mind and body?

In what ways does the Universe speak to you and give you personal signs and guidance?

What are you currently feeling inspired to do, create, or focus on in your life right now?

What is your relationship with taking time for rest and being still? Do you feel comfortable allowing yourself time to just *be* and do nothing? Why or why not?

Are there any fears or hurdles that block you from following the inspiration/guidance that is urging you to create something new or change paths?

ENERGY 5 - CREATIVE EXPLORATION

Flip to a blank page in this journal and grab something to draw with. Then, put on a favorite song, and draw or doodle whatever comes to mind while you're listening. Don't focus on the actual drawing, just get lost in the song and let it come out on the paper. Try this any time with your favorite songs, sound healing videos online, or even by putting a playlist on shuffle and drawing to whichever song plays at random.

Rub your earlobes and ears between your thumbs and forefingers with the intention of activating the energy centers and being open to hearing and listening to guidance. Do this as your sign and symbol to the Universe that you are listening and ready to hear!

Put on instrumental music and sit back, relax, and listen. Really tune in and try discerning one sound from another. What instruments do you hear in the music? Can you follow each one separately? Try this for a whole song or two, and see how challenging (or easy!) this is for you to do.

Ask Spirit, God, your Higher Self, or your Guides a question and request that the response be given in the highest light and for your highest good. Then, write a response to yourself as if you were speaking from their perspective. Don't worry about being wrong, just write the message. Note: Guidance is always kind and never harsh, harmful, or berating. So, if you begin to write something negative, know that it is ego and not guidance. Step away and say a prayer for clear and kind connection before you begin again.

ENERGY 6

Key concepts: intuition, vision, imagination,
prescience, knowing, perception,
and mental states

Element: Light | Rainbow Color: Purple | Musical Note: A

ENERGY 6 - AFFIRMATIONS

I am gifted with the magical ability of imagination.

I release worry about the timing of things; that is in the hands of the Universe.

Today, I trust in my own capacity to know what is right.

I am more than I was.

I allow myself to dream and play with different realities.

An oracle simply provides an answer that is already inside me.

The Light within me creates miracles in my life.

As I believe, so will it be for me, as my energy will attract its match in the outer world.

I have to endure the unknown and uncomfortable as I reinvent myself.

I absorb the lessons offered to me with grace.

ENERGY 6 - WRITING PROMPTS

What is the most repetitive sign you've been receiving from the Universe lately? What does this mean to you?

In your perception and experience, what lies beyond our material world? What are your views, thoughts, and impressions about what exists (or doesn't exist) beyond the physical world?

What did you dream of becoming as a child? Has that changed? What new dreams do you hold?

List five times in your life when seemingly coincidental events led you to an important change. Think about people you met "accidentally" or opportunities you learned about in the most unexpected and unusual way. Describe what happened. How did you feel?

What are the ideal changes you'd like to make, or goals you'd like to reach within the next year or so?

How does change make you feel? Are you energized and excited by it, or generally afraid of and resistant to it? Why?

ENERGY 6 - CREATIVE EXPLORATION

Draw a line down the middle of a blank page. On one half, draw your life as it is now and include all major details that stand out to you, including your thoughts and emotions. On the other half, draw your life as you desire it to be. What changed? Note: This is not an art project, and you do not have to be even remotely good at drawing. This is just a practice in bringing an energetic picture to life.

Focus on your breath. Breathe slowly and deeply until you feel relaxed. Let a landscape that represents your inner emotions arise in your mind's eye. Allow all your senses to take in its sights, smells, and sounds. What is the name of this place? What are the features of the landscape? What do you need to know about this place?

For the next week, focus on eating foods that are naturally vibrantly colored (so all your fruits and veggies!). You can focus on one color a day or try to get as much of the rainbow into your diet as possible every day. As you eat, imagine these natural foods strengthening the light and vitality of your body with their pure, vibrant, nourishing energy.

Bring your awareness to the center of your forehead, between your eyebrows. What sensations do you feel in this area? As you focus, notice a sphere of indigo energy—a deep, vibrant purple—begin to emerge. Take note of the quality of this energy. What size is it and how vibrant or muddy is the color? This is your Light of Intuition. Know that it is safe to see into the unseen and you are Divinely protected as you do so. Expand this energy center whenever you feel like strengthening your vision and intuition.

ENERGY 7

Key concepts: spirituality, ego transcendence, liberation,
God-consciousness, understanding,
and wisdom

Element: Thought | Rainbow Color: Golden White
| Musical Note: B

ENERGY 7 - AFFIRMATIONS

I am not separate from what I desire to manifest.

Expressing gratitude and asking to be of service is the most powerful, prospering prayer of all.

Surrendering truly will serve my highest good.

Spirit is always listening to me.

Spirit is my loving partner, reminding me that I am not alone.

I don't know what this sea of possibility has in store for me, so I stay curious and refrain from judgment or the need to label.

All manner of miracles are waiting for me to lay claim to them.

I let go of my struggle to find an answer and focus on other things for a while.

Life operates on Life's terms.

What is waiting for me lies beyond the ordinary.

ENERGY 7 - WRITING PROMPTS

What are some major realizations or epiphanies you've had in your life that have changed your path or deepened your spiritual experience?

In what ways are you being called to step out of your comfort zone right now?

Do you trust in life enough to step into the mysterious unknown and move forward? Do you seek definitive answers or reassurance from the Universe before even thinking about trusting enough to make your next move? Describe your general relationship with trust and surrender.

What is your relationship with prayer? How and when do you usually pray?

What synchronicities have you experienced in your life that really stand out to you as being more than "coincidences"?

Gratitude puts everything into perspective. List ten things that you are grateful for and the reason why. "*I'm grateful for . . . because . . .*"

Do you tend to take life experiences at face value, or do you seek a deeper spiritual meaning behind the things that occur? How does this perspective shape your choices and thoughts?

ENERGY 7 – CREATIVE EXPLORATION

Gather something to draw or paint with and find a bright, well-lit area to sit and create. Think about the relationship between you and your Higher Power: If it were a garden, what would it look like? Would it be full of vibrantly colored flowers and herbs or would it be full of poisonous plants and weeds? Would it feel safe and uplifting, or scary and unpredictable? Use a blank page or canvas to draw or paint a representation of your mind today.

Visit a library, bookstore, or your own bookshelf if you've got a pretty good collection. Go to a section that you feel drawn to, and choose a book "randomly" with the intention of hearing useful messages from Source—don't overthink this, just scan the shelf and grab whatever you feel called toward—and open it to whatever page you naturally land on. Read the page or the section you feel guided to. Spend some time doing this, and you'll be surprised at what useful and relevant pieces of information come through to help guide your path!

Close your eyes and take a few breaths. Bring your awareness to the crown of your head and notice any sensations you feel there. Picture sparkling white, Divine Light energy flowing down into your crown like water from a faucet, pouring down through your entire body, sending Divine Consciousness to every cell. What do you notice about the flow of this energy? Is the faucet set to just a light trickle or is it on full blast? Mentally adjust this flow to whatever pace feels correct for you. When the flow feels right and your spirit feels nourished, thank this constant flow of connection between you and Source; know that it is always there and can be adjusted whenever needed. Bring your awareness back into your body and back into the room, and open your eyes.

Today is a day when my
inspired ideas matter.

If I step back with clarity and
acceptance, I will realize that life is
offering me something magical.

I know that I
am enough.

When I feel the call
of the muse, I am being
invited to create.

I know that I
am enough.

If I step back with clarity and
acceptance, I will realize that life is
offering me something magical.

It's time to adjust the story
I tell about myself.

The Universe is inviting me to step
     into uncharted waters.

Love heals all
wounds, begins
all life.

No wish is
ever wasted.

Today is a day when my inspired ideas matter.

ORACLE

CARD SPREADS

Although there are many beautiful and complex spreads within oracle and tarot traditions, I personally find myself often turning to simple one-, two-, and three-card readings. I find they give you enough information to explore without overwhelming you with detail. I have included seven suggested interpretations you can use for your one-, two-, and three-card readings with the *Oracle of the 7 Energies* deck. (For the two- and three-card spreads, the meanings correspond with the card placements when read from left to right.) Use these spreads to explore the themes of each energy center and how they apply to your life.

1-CARD SPREADS

What do I need to know about the theme of this energy and how it plays out in my life today?

What do I need to release to move forward?

What do I need to know about my growth?

How do I realize my agenda?

What do I need in order to forgive fully?

How do I accept things as they come?

What do I need to do to bring more love to my life?

2-CARD SPREADS

Where am I now? / Where am I likely heading?

What should I focus on? / What am I learning?

What is going on? / What is hindering my progress?

How is this situation serving me? / What will I learn?

What is challenging? / How can I course correct?

What do I want from the relationship? / Where is the relationship heading?

What do I need to let go of? / What do I need to allow?

3-CARD SPREADS

Past / Present / Future

The nature of the problem / The cause / The solution

Opportunities / Challenges / Outcome

Option A / Option B / What do I need to know to make a decision?

What will help me? / What will hinder me? /
What is my unrealized potential?

Where I stand now / What I aspire to / How to get to my goal

What brings us together? / What pulls us apart? /
What needs my attention?

ENERGY MEDITATIONS

Stillness is one of the most powerful keys to tap into your intuition and experience more calm and happiness. While there are many ways to experience more stillness, I've found that meditation is one of the most effective. With meditation, you experience a clear conscious connection with the Divine and an open channel to your intuition.

I know meditation can be difficult for some people. When I first learned how to meditate, I felt uncomfortable, and I thought I would never still my busy mind. However, once I found the forms of meditation that worked best for me, I noticed an immediate stillness and calm.

I collaborated with my dear friend and talented musician, Erroll Starr Francis, to create a series of guided meditations, one meditation for each of the seven energy centers. I invite you to access these meditations when you want to take some time to be still, to focus on your breathing, and to connect with the Divine.

GET FREE ACCESS TO THE
ORACLE OF THE 7 ENERGIES MEDITATIONS AT:

Oracleofthe7Energies.com/Meditations

ENERGY 1 - MEDITATION

Meditation inspired by the element of earth moves you to feel more stable and grounded. Earth magic speaks to the intrinsic relationship that all living things have with the earth's consciousness. Meditating in this way will help you further connect to the energy of the earth while appealing to the quiet stillness within you. It will calm you and give you a sense of greater and higher purpose.

ENERGY 2 - MEDITATION

Water is all about intimacy and the willingness to be vulnerable. It's also about boundaries. When you meditate inspired by water, you encourage a greater self-understanding. This meditation will help you reflect on yourself, how you connect with others, and how your limits are sacred.

ENERGY 3 - MEDITATION

When you meditate based on the energy of Fire, you are moving consciously and with purpose. Step into your power and watch all of your intentions manifest into the world. Fire Energy tells you that change can be a positive driving force in your life. You do not need to fear change.

ENERGY 4 - MEDITATION

Love Energy teaches you to give and accept forgiveness. When you meditate inspired by Love Energy, it helps you accept that you are responsible for how you see the world. If your perception, your judgment, or your reactions are awry, then meditation can help you open up your heart and let go.

ENERGY 5 - MEDITATION

Sound Energy opens you to new information and invokes the spirit of creative expression. Get creative, feel inspired, and truly listen with a meditation inspired by Sound Energy. This will help you understand and accept that you do not have to do everything yourself!

ENERGY 6 - MEDITATION

Meditations inspired by Light Energy encourage you to see, accept, and acknowledge all your potential. Anything you imagine has the potential to become real. Moving toward Divine vision begins with opening yourself up further, and this meditation can help you.

ENERGY 7 - MEDITATION

Thought Energy will liberate you. This meditation inspired by Thought Energy will move you toward an expression of deep and authentic gratitude as you connect to Divine consciousness. It will also help you be at peace and know that all your prayers will be answered. Expressing gratitude can be the most powerful prayer of all, moving you toward experiencing the unity of all things.

GET FREE ACCESS TO THE
ORACLE OF THE 7 ENERGIES MEDITATIONS AT:

Oracleofthe7Energies.com/Meditations

ABOUT THE AUTHOR

Colette Baron-Reid is a leader in the field of personal transformation, practical spirituality, and intuition. Her best-selling books and oracle cards are published worldwide in 27 languages. She is the founder of Oracle School, a global online learning experience with students in 36 countries, where self-empowerment, co-creation, and ancient oracles meet in a contemporary way. Colette is also the creator of the energy psychology technique the Invision Process®.

Colette is the author of *Remembering the Future; Messages from Spirit; The Map; Uncharted*; and the popular oracle decks and apps *The Wisdom of Avalon, Wisdom of the Hidden Realms, The Enchanted Map, Wisdom of the Oracle, Postcards from Spirit, Mystical Shaman Oracle, Goddess Power Oracle, Spirit Animal Oracle, Crystal Spirits Oracle*, and more. She divides her time between Canada and the United States with her husband and three funny little Pomeranians.

Visit her at **colettebaronreid.com**.

ALSO BY COLETTE BARON-REID

Books

The Map

Messages from Spirit

Remembering the Future

Uncharted

Card Decks

The Crystal Spirits Oracle

The Enchanted Map Oracle Cards

Goddess Power Oracle
(standard and deluxe editions)

The Good Tarot

The Mystical Shaman Oracle
(with Alberto Villoldo and Marcela Lobos)

The Oracle of E (with Pam Grout)

Oracle of the 7 Energies

Postcards from Spirit

The Spirit Animal Oracle

The Wisdom of Avalon Oracle Cards

Wisdom of the Hidden Realms

Wisdom of the Oracle Divination Cards